Copyright © 2025 by Ed Boxall

All rights reserved. No part of this publication may be reproduced, stored or transmitted in any form or by any means, electronic, mechanical, photocopying, recording, scanning, or otherwise without written permission from the publisher. It is illegal to copy this book, post it to a website, or distribute it by any other means without permission.

First edition

Published By
The Pearbox Press,
50 Edmund Road
Hastings
UK
TN35 5LF

Edboxall.co.uk

Pearbox Books

For Rachel, Sammy, Flynn and all the children and staff at Seymour Primary Academy, Crawley where I love being artist in residence.

Lily

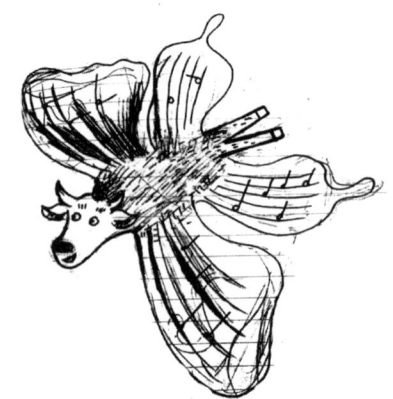

Ruby

Off with his Nose	6
Mr Jefferies	8
Place of Many Moons	16
Miss Cripps	20
Wizard	29
Miss Thursday	33
Regrets	42
Busy Socks	48
Not Fair	51
Digging Up Evidence	59
The President	63
The Ring	68
Rumours	70
Bullying Holes	73
Brave Decision	78
Shock	83
Um…	87
It All Comes Out	93
Funny Friends	97
The Journey On	101

Mr Codd

Mr Hipkin

Mrs Standhope

James

Miss Thursday

Miss Cripps

A. Fox

Moses

Mr Jefferies

Arousha Iman Beth

Off with his Nose!

Lily Smith sat in class at 9 o'clock on Monday morning. She was waiting for her teacher to arrive. She was also wondering *who* her teacher would be.

You see, Lily's normal teacher, Mr Hipkin, was away. He was off with his nose.

I don't mean he'd gone off on holiday with his nose. His nose wasn't sunbathing next to him on a tiny deck chair. That would be silly.

What I mean is this. Mr Hipkin had broken his nose while skateboarding and was staying at home until it was better. Everyone in class had been saying 'He's off with his nose' because it sounded funny.

So, the class were going to have a supply teacher until he came back. The supply teacher was late and everyone was very busy.

Finn and Joe were busy laughing at something on Joe's phone.

Harry and Megan were busy playing tag.

James was busy playing air guitar.

Arousha, Beth and Iman were busy seeing who could stand on their head the longest.

And Ruby was busy putting something nasty in Mr Hipkin's desk drawer as a surprise for the new teacher.

Lily Smith just wanted everyone to be good so the class didn't get in trouble.

All of a sudden there was a shout above the noise "Stop this at once or it's detention for everyone!"

Everyone looked to the doorway to see who had shouted.

"Only joking dudes!" Said their supply teacher as he turned on the flashing lights on his heart-shaped glasses. "Mr Jefferies has arrived! Form a line for selfies please"

Mr Jefferies, along with his guitar, heart shaped glasses, and big smile strode into the room.

Mr Jefferies

Mr Jefferies started the day by taking the register while playing his guitar. He got everyone to sing their name back. So, he sang:

'Hello Jemma Abbot, Jemma are you here' in a sing song voice.

And then Jemma had to sing-

'I am Jemma, I am here'.

Mr Jefferies was really trying to make things fun. And it worked. To start with. Some of the children at the start of the register like Mohammad Badje and Mara Boxall enjoyed singing back. But it took SO long to do the whole register that by the time it got to Robert Jones and Kirsty

Lime people were getting bored and fidgety, which was making Mr Jefferies grumpy.

Lily got more and more worried about singing as they went through the register. And when Lily was worried, she scrunched her whole face up and blinked. She blinked and blinked and blinked and couldn't stop. The more worried she got, the more she blinked. So she was blinking a lot by the time Mr Jefferies got to her name in the register. When it was finally Lily's turn to sing, the words wouldn't come out. Mr Jefferies snapped 'Come on Lily Smith! Let's get this done!" and she managed to whisper-sing. "I am Lily, I am here" and felt like she might cry.

After musical-registration Mr Jefferies explained he was a singer in a rock band. He talked about how he'd once been on a programme called Top of The Pops in his band The Shadow Crows.

He seemed disappointed no one in class had heard of Top of The Pops or The Shadow Crows.

By morning break they had spent:

1. 20 minutes doing register,
2. 40 minutes listening to Mr Jefferies introducing himself
3. absolutely no time on work at all.

After break, Mr Jefferies gave them all an easy maths task that they got done quickly. So he said 'just read a book or do some drawing'. This meant some kids read a book or did a drawing and other kids messed about. Lily did a drawing of a princess that she tried to show Mr Jefferies but he was busy showing James and Amir his guitar. Lily was miserable. All the messing about made her really anxious. She didn't like people moving around all the time or sudden noises like when someone shouted. Worst of all, Ruby had started teasing her by copying her nervous blinking. Some of Ruby's friends were joining in.

Mr Hipkin would have stopped them picking on her. He always noticed those sort of things. But Mr Jefferies didn't notice at all.

Throughout the school day Mr Jefferies got grumpier and grumpier and shoutier and shoutier. The heart shaped glasses and big smile had gone by lunch.

The headteacher, Mrs Standhope walked in to check on the class at 2:30.

At the moment Mrs Standhope walked in there were bits of paper everywhere, and James was standing on a chair playing air guitar. Mr Jefferies had just found out what Ruby had left for him in the desk drawer. His hand was in the air with green slime dripping onto the carpet. It did not make a good impression on Mrs Standhope.

By the end of the day Mr Jefferies looked like this:

He never came back to Bogwood School.

Place of Many Moons

That night Lily dreamt she was walking,

Over hills of soft green grass,

Rosy warm moons shone above,

And buttercows fluttermooed past.

A breeze of cool summer mornings,

Brushed gently over her face,

She knew she was the first person,

In this newly created place.

She had a funny feeling,

There was *something* she really must do,

She needed to find the perfect spot,

To make *something* special and new.

She saw a wizard in the distance,

So she called out "Hey wizard hello!",

she asked him 'what should I make here?'

He answered "I can't find my nose!"

At that moment a hundred alarm clocks,

Blasted up out of the ground,

She was in bed, and it was time to get up,

And her dream drifted off with the clouds.

Miss Cripps

Mr Jefferies was replaced by Miss Cripps.

Maths started out well.

She got everyone working so there wasn't much messing about.

But as the lesson went on, Lily realised Miss Cripps was basically just working with Arousha, Beth and Iman. Those 3 shared a table and were the best at everything. Miss Cripps was so excited about how good those three were at maths that she forget about the rest of class. Slowly but surely the class got more and more badly behaved as children got bored.

Miss Cripps didn't notice the pencils flying through the air, or the secret mobile phones that had appeared on knees under tables, or James and Amir trying to crawl under all the chairs without being seen. She was completely focussed on finding more and more difficult equations for Arousha, Beth and Iman. Lily heard her say "Yes! GOALLL!" every time one of them got a maths question right.

Lily was stuck on her maths and felt bored and anxious. She was blinking a lot.

Luckily, Ruby was joining in with James and Amir on their under-chair adventure, so at least she wasn't picked on Lily about her blinking.

This was when she noticed her castle by the sink in the art area. It was a project she'd started a while ago when Mr Hipkin was there. She had been building a medieval castle out of old cardboard tubes, boxes and masking tape for a history project. There were lots of other castles that other children had made in little groups. But Mr Hipkin knew she liked to work on her own. So it was just *her* castle. She remembered the class as it was when they'd been making the castles. She'd been so absorbed and happy working on her castle, while Mr Hipkin had put on some gentle music. It was a nice memory.

It was obvious Miss Cripps wasn't interested in what anyone but the three geniuses were doing so Lily went over and looked at her castle. She made a little space by the sink to work and started mending a turret that had got broken. The bell went for break. Lily wanted to put a bit more tape on to fix the broken turret so she didn't go out. No one was meant to stay in class at break but she was enjoying the quiet and didn't want to go out to the busyness of the playground. So, she stayed inside and worked on her castle all the way through break. No one noticed she hadn't been out to play.

The rest of the day carried on in a similar way. In literacy, Miss Cripps set them a task, everyone worked well for a while and then Miss Cripps worked with the kids who were best at English and forgot about everyone else. She shouted " YESSS! 15 adjectives and a clear understanding of onomatopoeia! RESULT!!", high fived Beth and did a little dance like when a footballer scores a goal.

Lily went back to her castle whenever she could. She knew she wasn't doing what she was meant to but she hated sitting and waiting. And she hated everyone moving around where they shouldn't and all the shouting and giggling. She liked her little safe place building the castle.

I bet some of you are thinking 'Why didn't Lily just enjoy messing about like the rest of class? It sounds like fun". The thing is messing about wasn't fun for Lily. It just worried her. She had no idea why everyone laughed when Mr Jefferies put his hand in that slime. She could only think "'Is he going to get angry or start crying? That would be horrible".And she had no idea why James and Amir found it so funny crawling around with chairs stuck on their backs saying 'potato' over and again. Why on earth would you laugh about something when someone could get in trouble or get hurt?

Now, Lily did laugh at some things. She laughed at TV programmes that were supposed to be a bit young for her. She still laughed at Mr Tumble. And she loved funny animal videos. She had watched a YouTube clip of a cat that sounds like it's barking like a dog 37 times. If something was on kid's TV or kid's YouTube you knew nothing was going to go badly wrong.

But for now, in class, it seemed like a hundred different things could go wrong.

So instead of joining in the chaos of the classroom, she worked on her castle. It was starting to look good.

At lunch break, she ate her packed lunch and snuck back into class to work on her castle.

In the afternoon, Ruby sat down next to Lily and said "Where have you been?" We needed you for chasing game. The teams weren't even."

Lily whispered, with her head down, "I felt ill so sat in class" trying not to blink. But of course she did.

"Poor Blinksy" said Ruby and started blinking really hard to copy Lily. She knew it would make Lily blink more. Lily felt awful and so blinked more. And that made Ruby blink more. Lily hated this. This was a game that Ruby enjoyed a lot, especially when Ruby's friends joined in the bullying. Lily hated it.

Everyone knows you should tell a grown up if you're bullied. But Lily couldn't tell anyone. The words just wouldn't come out. Going up to a teacher and saying 'I'm being bullied' felt as hard as climbing Mount Everest barefoot. Or building a real actual castle on your own.

At last Miss Cripps came back. It was PE in the afternoon.

During PE Ruby secretly blinked nastily at Lily whenever Miss Cripps wasn't looking in her direction.

So now Lily did something she had never done before. She lied to a teacher. She went up to Miss Cripps and said 'I feel sick' and was sent to the office.

Lily was always good so Mrs Kapadia, the school secretary, didn't think she could be lying. She called home for her mum to take her home but there was no answer.

"Do you think you could go back to class? Perhaps sit quietly and do something you enjoy." said Mrs Kapadia.

"I think so..." said Lily in her smallest I-think-I-could-if-I'm-really-brave voice.

And that was how Lily got to spend Tuesday afternoon working happily on her castle while the rest of the class did PE outside in the rain. She had a bucket with a plastic bag in it next to her that Mrs Kapadia had given her in case she was sick. She felt a tiny weeny bit guilty for lying. But she also felt something she'd never felt before...she was excited about getting away with doing something wrong. It felt good to be a little bit bad.

Wizard

That night Lily's dream continued.

The wizard walked up with a grin.

She recognised his kind laughing eyes,

And said "Hello Mr Hipkin!"

His nose fluttered around him,

On wizzing butterfly wings,

As he pointed towards a flat empty hill,

And said 'now it's time to begin'

He said 'Build a castle!

A place to hide and be safe,

The rooms will be filled with furturglly things,

To help you be strong, kind, and brave.

She smiled politely at her teacher,
Though she didn't understand all he'd said
He turned into a firework and filled up the sky
With yellow and pink, green and red.

Down where he had pointed she saw,
Her *socks* were carrying stones,
To her t-shirts who were building the walls,
And her jumper was digging the moat.

Soon her clothes had built a castle,
With towers and higgledy roofs,
But the moons turned into alarm clocks,
She woke up, and got ready for school.

Miss Thursday

The teacher for Wednesday was Miss Thursday.

This of course made everyone laugh.

But the laughing didn't last long. Miss Thursday gave the class a mean look that seemed to make an icy wind blow through the classroom. There was no laughter in Miss Thursday's class.

When the children had arrived they'd found the class had been re-organised so all the tables were in rows so you had to sit alone looking forwards. Like pictures of schools in Victorian times. On each table there was a pile of worksheets, a sharp pencil and a pencil sharpener. There was also a piece of paper with a type written 'List of No's'. Some of the No's were very odd:

No fighting

No coloured socks

No black socks

No singing

No eggs

No moving out of seat without permission

No going to the toilet during lesson time

No complaining

No witch craft

No rubber bands

No make up

No pets or parents

No string

No stink bombs

No x ray glasses

No frisbees

No poking

No sticks

No burping

No slime

No spiders

No rubber spiders

No scab picking

No nose blowing in class

The same rules were up on the smart board at the front.

I bet you're thinking "That'll never work! People will just break the rules.' But there was something about Miss Thursday that made you stick to the rules. She looked at you in a way that made you feel like you were a mouse about to be eaten by a cat. So you froze. Dead still. And hoped she'd go away and eat someone else. It was like a kind of super power.

So, through the morning everyone sat in silence and did their worksheets while Miss Thursday paced slowly up and down.

The morning felt very long and boring. But even Ruby was terrified of Miss Thursday. So at least Lily was free from being bullied.

At break time, Miss Thursday made everyone tuck their seats under their desks carefully before they went out.

But once they were outside they were like 31 restless dogs who had just been let out of a car after being shut up for hours on a long journey.

They whooped and ran and got into argued and bumped into each other. There were lots of tears and red faces.

Even Lily joined in with chasing game. After sitting still for so long she didn't feel like working on her castle. For some reason Ruby wasn't there so Lily actually enjoyed joining in.

The bell rang and they all reluctantly lined up to go back inside to Miss Thursday.

When they got back to class Lily glanced at her castle. She gasped and the tears rushed up in her eyes. The towers were all torn off, the walls were torn to pieces and all her careful brick work was scribbled on. Someone had even thrown glitter on it. The class weren't even allowed glitter. The castle was ruined.

She forgot about Miss Thursday's rules and ran towards her poor broken castle.

"Stop right there!" shouted Mrs Thursday so loudly everyone jumped.

Lily couldn't bring herself to tell Miss Thursday what had happened. Miss

Thursday pointed at Lily's seat and glared at her with those terrible killer-cat eyes. Lily sat down, the tears just held back from falling.

She knew it had been Ruby who had trashed her castle. She must have done it at break while she had been away from chasing game. It must have only taken her a moment to destroy what had taken her hours to make. Lily was blinking a lot. With anger now. She had had enough. She would do something. She would find a way to hurt Ruby. It wasn't fair.

"Lily Smith. Your turn"

It was Miss Thursday. Lily hadn't been listening. Everyone in class were taking it in turns to read out from a book called 'The Secret Garden'. Lily hadn't been following the story because she was so upset.

She didn't even know where the last person had got to in the book.

"Lily Smith. Your turn. Stand up and read"

She stood up and blinked and didn't say anything.

"Useless! Sit down and come to me for detention at lunchtime"

This was the first detention Lily had ever had. The first time she had ever been in trouble.

At detention, Lily had to sit and read a whole page of The Secret Garden to Miss Thursday while she marked worksheets and took no notice of her at all.

After she had finished Miss Thursday said, "Off you go now. Try harder next time" and Lily walked away through the empty school towards the playground. It was empty because everyone was outside in the sunshine. She walked by where the year 5 coats and bags were hung up. She walked towards the door to the playground and stopped. There was Ruby's bag, covered in heart patterns.

She unzipped it. She reached inside. She expected to find a pencil case. Perhaps an empty packed lunch box. But her fingers wrapped around Ruby's mobile phone. It was one of the really expensive ones. She quickly put it in her pocket. It was as if her fingers had stolen it without her mind knowing. She quickly put it in her own bag. She walked outside. Her heart raced.

All afternoon Lily was terrified of being found out. But, by some miracle, Ruby didn't realise her phone had gone until she got home.

Regrets

That evening, Lily felt awful. She was terrified of getting in trouble about the phone. This would be serious trouble. Definitely parents-coming-into-school trouble. Perhaps an exclusion. She had gone from never doing anything wrong at school to getting a detention and stealing a mobile phone worth £300 in one day. £300! She felt sick with worry. She might be in trouble with the police. Would they send her to prison? She'd heard that if you get a criminal record you can never get a job when you're older. Oh WHY had she done it??

The thing was, mixed up with all these worries she was pleased that Ruby would be really, really upset. Because day after day after day Ruby bullied her about her blinking.

When Lily was alone in her room she got the phone out and looked at it. It was so strange to see it in her room. Something in the wrong place. Like a piece of alien technology had appeared in her room. And then it rang. She jumped. She quickly pressed the red 'cancel call' button and turned it off. Luckily her mum and dad hadn't heard. It took a very long time for her heart to slow down to its normal speed.

While they were eating dinner Lily thought up a plan.

Later, while her mum was watching TV and her dad was putting her little brother Moses to bed, Lily went outside into the garden. The phone was in her pocket. She swung on the swing for a minute, just to seem normal in case anyone saw her. And then she went into the shed and got one of her dad's trowels. She found a spot on the edge of lawn under the brambles and dug a hole as quickly and as deep as she could. She placed the phone in the hole, filled it up with earth, and put a bit of turf on top. She made it look as if nothing had changed. She quickly put the trowel away and went back to the swing.

She took a long, long time getting to sleep that night. She worried that someone had found out that she'd stolen Ruby's phone. She worried that her parents would stop thinking she was a good person. She worried she'd get excluded from school. She worried she'd get in trouble with the police. She worried that Ruby had realised it was her.

The worries got bigger and bigger and raced around her head, as the hours passed very very slowly. She saw 2:15 glowing on her clock but somehow she fell asleep soon after that.

Busy Socks

She found her clothes had been busy,

While she had been working at school.

The castle was as big as a city,

Beneath the warm rosy lights of the moons.

Her shoes and socks sung like birds,

And played tag with her scarf in the sky,

As she meandered over the rooftops,

In the moonfragrant shimmersoft night.

So perfectly peaceful and calm,

She wanted to stay there always,

But as usual her dream came to an end,

her alarm clock shocked her awake.

Not Fair

Lily woke up to her dad at the door saying:

" Wake up Lily! Those foxes have been back. They've been digging up my lawn again"

Foxes. In the garden. Digging. THE PHONE!!!

Lily sprung up and ran out the room and then slowed down so she didn't looked look suspicious. She hadn't thought of the *foxes* when she buried the phone. Now and again foxes visited her garden in the night and dug holes in the lawn looking for worms.

Sure enough, the lawn was covered in little shallow holes. Lily was usually excited to see these holes. She loved the idea of foxes visiting secretly in the night. But of course this morning she could only think about whether those foxes had dug up the phone. She could see a hole near where she had buried the phone. They hadn't quite reached it. Thank Goodness. Lily new she would have to dig up the phone herself and hide it somewhere else in case the foxes came back. But her mum and Moses were playing in the garden so she didn't get a chance before school.

The first thing Lily saw when she went into school that day was Ruby coming into school with her mum. Her mum looked furious. Ruby and her mum went in to see Mrs Standhope. Everyone who went near Mrs Standhope's office could hear Ruby's mum shouting angrily.

It soon got round the rest of the class that Ruby's phone had been stolen. People were putting their arms around Ruby's shoulder and saying nice things to her. They felt sorry for her because she'd lost her phone but also because they knew how much trouble she was in with her mum and dad. They were also saying horrible things about whoever had stolen it. *It wasn't supposed to be like this* thought Lily.

All day long she worried about whether her dad would find the phone when he filled in the foxholes.

And all day long she worried that Ruby would find out she stole the phone.

She even had the funny feeling that she would blurt out "it was me! I stole it!" without meaning to.

So, with all these worries of course she blinked worse than ever.

And so Ruby picked on her worse than ever.

So she blinked worse than ever.

But at least it seemed Ruby had no idea it was her who had stolen her phone. After all Ruby often teased her for being being good and never getting into trouble. She said things to her like 'Lily goody goody shiny shoes' with 'perfect Mummy and Daddipoos'. Ruby clearly thought that Lily would be the last person on earth to steal her phone.

There was a special assembly about the crime. Mrs Standhope talked a lot about how the thief should be brave and own up. She said they wouldn't get in so much trouble if they were honest now. Lily noticed that she didn't say they wouldn't get in *any* trouble. Just that they wouldn't get in *so much* trouble. Ruby was right about something: Lily *was* a goody goody shiny shoes. She was terrified of getting in any trouble at all.

So Lily was not going to own up. She'd got away with it. And there was no reason to think that would change, as long as no one found the phone.

But, during the day something awful happened.

Some of the kids in class decided *James* had stolen the phone. They thought this because he was often in trouble. He got in trouble for getting angry and swearing when he felt he was being treated unfairly. But he'd never stolen anything. But, the rumour got round it was him. Like most rumours it was a complete mystery who had started it.

At lunch, Lily could see James was pacing along the fence banging it with a stick looking angrily round at the playground. Unfairness was the thing that made him more angry than anything else. And it was *so* unfair he was being blamed for stealing the phone.

She could tell he was going to lose control and swear or throw chairs or knock over a table. If that happened, James might be excluded from school for good. He was on his last chance. He had nearly been permanently excluded so many times. Once more and that would be it. And it would be her fault.

Lily walked towards James to be friendly and try to calm him down. But she didn't get to him. Before she got there she suddenly felt really shy and walked into school instead and started trying to fix her castle.

***

At the end of the day, Lily saw that Ruby's mum was still really angry when she came to pick Ruby up. Lily saw Ruby with her head down, looking at her feet as she walked home. She could hear her mum talking angrily. "That phone cost £300. I was so stupid to trust you with it at school. You will be paying me back every

penny out of your pocket money " Ruby didn't reply at all. Lily had never seen Ruby looking so weak and sad before.

She felt a bit sorry for Ruby.

And she felt so horribly sorry for James she felt sick. She knew she could stop the rumour that he'd stolen the phone if she owned up. But she couldn't. She just couldn't. She'd be in *so* much trouble.

That wasn't meant to happen thought Lily.

She was blinking so much that she went home with horribly achy dry eyes and a headache.

Digging up Evidence

When Lily got home she was relieved to see that all the mess that the foxes had left behind was still there. Her dad hadn't been out there yet. She would still be able to dig up the phone as long as her dad didn't get there first. However, just as she was hanging up her coat her dad appeared with a rake and a spade and said "I'm off to tidy up that mess those pesky foxes left behind". Lily thought quickly and said "I'll do it Dad". Lily grabbed the spade and rake and spent an hour tidying up the mess. "You're such a lovely kid" said her dad. 'If only you knew the truth' thought Lily.

Unfortunately, her mum and dad were in the kitchen and Moses was playing on the back step the whole time she was tidying up so she never got a chance to dig up the phone.

So, she had another plan.

When she was in bed she made herself stay awake until everyone else was asleep.

She crept downstairs into the garden. The moon was full in the sky. So bright it was almost like daylight. She thought about how there was just one moon in our world. What a strange thought. She quickly went into the shed and got the trowel. She found the place where she was sure she had buried the phone. She dug. No phone. She dug just nearby. No phone. Her fast frantic breathing sounded very loud in the silent night. She dug another hole. Surely she was in the right place this time? No phone. She started to think perhaps she'd dreamt burying the phone. She ended up digging seven holes before at last she found it.

She quickly threw the phone in the outside bin and went inside. But there was her dad. Sleepy, in his pyjamas. "I heard a noise- What on earth are you doing Lily?" he said. "I heard the fox so I went out to see" Lily replied. "They've just gone. I'm afraid they've messed up our garden again."

She got into bed. Her racing heart kept her awake for a long time.

It wasn't me!

The President of the World

Lily was back on top of her castle.
She noticed a little old door.
She opened it wide and stepped inside
And walked down a long corridor.

There were rooms on each side, full of old junk-
a humungous lost property store.
"furturgly things" she said to herself,
And kicked a deflated football.

There were stuffed giraffes, school books, wigs,
Water bottles and chairs,
Bird cages, mowers, lampshades, plugs,
and bald one eyed teddy bears.

'I wonder who all this belonged to '

She thought, and felt sad and strange,

Like she might be lost property too,

So she turned back to the rooftops again.

But the corridors narrowed, ceilings pushed down,

She could only get through with a squeeze,

She opened a door, found herself on a stage,

Where a crowd expected her speech.

She realised then, with a loud gasp,

That she was president of the whole world.

She was pleased she woke up in her own bed,

To find she was still just a girl.

The Ring

Her mum woke her up, saying 'Wake up Lily. I need your help. I've lost my wedding ring!"

Her mum was in tears. She said "I'm going to search the bin outside for it. Could you look under the sofa?"

"Don't worry Mum. I'll do the bin." She had to get that phone before her mum.

And so, before she went to school Lily ended up tipping out the whole outdoor bin and getting covered in left over blobs of yoghurt, the yucky dregs from tins of tomatoes, and old soggy coffee grounds. But, she did find the phone and put it in her pocket. No wedding ring though. She went to her room and shoved the phone at the bottom of her box of cuddly toys. Not a great hiding place but it would have to do for now. She had to have an extra shower as she was so dirty. As she was standing in the shower, she saw something shiny behind the shampoo bottle. It was Mum's wedding ring.

Rumours

At School, the rumour about James stealing the phone was still going round. In fact, it had evolved in the strange way that rumours do. Some children were passing it on to each other as if it was fact. Even very sensible children like Mohammed and Beth and Iman we're starting to believe it. Ruby didn't totally believe this rumour. She liked James and often played with him. But she didn't completely *not* believe it either. So, she found herself staying out of his way not quite sure what to do, hoping the real thief would be found so she could be sure it wasn't James. Rumours really are horrible things. AVOID THEM.

However, sometimes people who really should know better believe them. Mr Codd, the deputy head, was one of those people. He heard the rumour while he was on playground duty. And he believed it. And he wanted to impress Mrs Standhope by solving the crime. Mr Codd loved those crime shows where police interrogate suspects in little bare windowless rooms. He decided to interrogate poor innocent James.

So, in the afternoon, Mr Codd came into class while they were reading from The Secret Garden and asked to see James. James went off with Mr Codd. In a few minutes Lily heard James running through the school, pulling over chairs as he went. She also heard him shout something I'm not allowed to write. "I didn't ****ing steal it!".

Mr Codd had asked James if he had stolen it in that tough-guy-TV-detective way that sounded like he'd already decided he was guilty. Nothing made James angrier than being accused unfairly so he had sworn at Mr Codd. Lily knew how worried James was about getting in trouble. James dreaded that he would be permanently excluded.

By the end of the day Lily had been blinking so hard that she had a horrible headache and every muscle in her face was screwed up.

Bully Holes

Lily was back on that horrible stage,

And was still President of the World,

Miss Cripps shouted from the audience,

"You're just an average girl!

And you are a RUBBISH president!

You're not as good as Iman!"

Lily's eyelids blinked like furious wings,

The audience cruelly laughed.

Their blinks were an army of scissors,

Their laughter was cackling drills.

But something changed in Lily.

Her eyelids were suddenly still.

"STOP" said Lily. "ENOUGH!"

"I'm your president. That is TUBOLE

And magoogle is turt and Charles is my toe,

And doughnuts no longer have holes!"

The audience were silent. Then stood up and cheered.

Lily waved as she walked off the stage.

She went out through a door, to a room, with a floor,

Full of holes with a lot of complaints.

They screamed "DOUGHNUTS NEED HOLES!

We need a new president, Lily must go!"

Louder and louder. In Ruby's voice now

"Down with Blinky! Lily must go!"

"Down with Blinky! Lily must go!"
"Down with Blinky! Lily must go!"
"Down with Blinky! Lily must go!"
"Down with Blinky! Lily must go!"

But from across the room, she could hear,
The sound of her radio at home,
She knew she must reach it, to escape this place,
Full of snarkingly snide bully holes.

But she stepped, she tripped with a dizzying sink,
Down a hole with a nasty cruel snigger,
But she held onto the edge and saved herself,
With her amazingly strong little finger.

So strong in fact, she pulled herself up,

And out of that bullying hole.

She sat up with a gasp and was happily back,

In her cosy warm bed back at home.

Now she could hear from the kitchen below,

A friendly radio show,

And her dream of the castle, and the bullying holes,

drifted away like dreamsmoke.

Brave Decision

Lily woke up in her bed to the sound of the radio playing downstairs in the kitchen. She wiggled her little finger. It still hurt a bit from pulling her out of the hole. 'I have so much strength in just my little finger' thought Lily as she tried to hold onto the memory of the dream. "I can climb out of any bully hole". But after a moment she had forgotten it completely.

She woke up and checked for the phone in her box of teddies. She noticed her teddies were messed up, one or two were missing. And the phone was gone.

She frantically looked all around her room. No phone. She thought that her mum must have found the phone. Lily was at last going to be in big trouble.

When she walked into the kitchen she was expecting to see the phone on the table and her mum and dad waiting to tell her off. But no. Mum was happily unloading the dishwasher and Dad was outside trying to figure out how to protect the garden from those pesky foxes.

Everything was normal. Apart from one thing. Moses was tugging on her arm and saying "presents! presents!" On the kitchen table she could see the soft shapes of lots of her cuddlies wrapped in layers and layers of brown paper and masking tape. You see, one of Moses' favourite games was wrapping ordinary things up and giving them as presents. Cute. He'd gone into Lily's room while she was asleep and borrowed lots of her cuddlies and wrapped them up as presents to give back to her. One of those presents didn't look like a cuddly. It looked a lot like a very expensive mobile phone wrapped up in lots of layers of brown paper and masking tape.

Lily said to Moses "Oh thank you so much! Let's have a special party in my room" They went up to her room and she opened up the package with her purple octopus in it. "We'll open the rest later, I promise" she said. She put the wrapped up phone in her pocket without Moses noticing.

She had made a big decision. She had had enough. Enough of trying to get rid of this phone that just did not seem to want to go anywhere. Enough of worrying about Ruby finding out about her crime. Enough of worrying about James getting in trouble and being excluded from school because of her. Enough of this headache and blinking.

She went into the toilet and unwrapped the phone. Amazingly it still looked in good

condition despite the mud, the worms, a night in a stinky bin, and being wrapped up by a four year old.

Today, Ruby would get her phone back.

Shock

Lily left a little bit early for school because she planned to give Ruby the phone before school to get it over with. On the way it felt like the phone was made of some alien material that let out a strange magnetic power. It was as if people would somehow know it was there.

When she got to school she saw Ruby with her friends sitting on the tables in class laughing. She suddenly didn't dare tell her. It felt an impossible thing to do so she hung her bag up on the hooks in the hallway. All morning she felt that phone there in her bag as if it was calling out to be discovered. She decided during numeracy lesson that she would go and tell Mrs Standhope about the phone instead of telling Ruby. She'd explain. She would be in trouble but Mrs Standhope would understand. She was always fair. She wouldn't tell the police. Or would she? No, she would be in trouble but it would be okay. It would be the beginning of this horrible time being over. The beginning of getting back to normal. Hopefully.

So, at break time she went to her bag when no one was around and took out the phone and put it in her pocket. The pockets on her school dress were small. If someone had looked straight at her pocket they would have seen the shape of that phone. She walked to Mrs Standhope's office. She passed other kids as if everything was normal. But things were not normal. Lily, the girl you never did anything wrong was about to own up to doing the naughtiest thing that anyone in her class had ever done. The phone seemed to get heavier and heavier and she blinked more and more and more. She got to the office. She looked through the window expecting to see Mrs Standhope sitting at her computer. She expected her to smile and wave and ask her to come in, in the friendly way she always did. But it wasn't Mrs Standhope at the computer. It was Mr Codd. There was no way she was owning up to Mr Codd. No way. She turned around just as the bell for the end of break time rang. She had no time to put the phone back in her bag. She was stuck with it in her pocket. A small pocket where anyone could see it if they looked. A pocket it could easily fall out of.

She couldn't concentrate at all during literacy. She sat in a strange way with her leg stretched out to make the phone less likely it would fall out. And she checked her pocket all the time. It was amazing no one noticed. At last, at lunch, she went to put the phone back in her bag. But it was impossible. There were kids everywhere.

She couldn't just wait around looking suspicious until everyone went.

She had another idea. If no one was in class she could put the phone in Mr Hipkin's desk drawer. Maybe she could even shove it right to the back so no one would find it for a long time.

But when she got to class, someone was there. The last person she wanted to see. Ruby. And she was standing over her castle.

Um...

Lily wasn't shy now. 'What are you doing?" said Lily angrily. Ruby looked round as Lily ran over to her.

Lily expected to see her castle even more broken. But Ruby had the masking tape and scissors out and was *fixing* it.

"Hello, I'm working on the castle."

said Ruby.

"It's not *the* castle. It's **MY** castle." Said Lily

"Alright blinky. I didn't realise. I worked on it the other day at playtime when I was bored of chasing game."

Lily was hot all over. Her heart was beating fast. Her fingers tingled. And she found now she had started speaking the words were pouring out her like a tap that was turned on full.

"Lily is my name. Not Blinky. And this castle is mine. You didn't work on it. You came in and trashed it. I know you did"

"No I didn't. I worked on it. I tried to make it better. But then I couldn't get things to stick properly and well…yes…I guess I did sort of trash it a little bit 'cos I got angry. It was driving me mad. I'm rubbish at cutting and sticking"

"I don't believe you. You came in and deliberately broke it. You did it to bully me. Like you always do."

" I don't bully you"

"Yes you do. You copy me blinking. And you call me blinky. And you call me things like Shiny Sparkle Goody Poo Shoes. And YOU TRASHED MY CASTLE."

"That's not bullying. It's just having fun. And you ARE shiny sparkle poo bum sparkle shoes. You never do *anything* wrong."

" What's so good about doing things wrong?? The clues in the word- WRONG! And It's not fun when you say those things. I hate it"

"Okay, well I'll stop then. Doesn't bother me. But it's not bullying. I'm not a bully"

"Yes you are"

"I'm not"

"Yes you are. And it's MY castle."

"I just thought it could do with a little bling. I found the glitter."

"We're not allowed the glitter"

"Well I know where it is- in the top cupboard. I got it"

"That's stealing" Lily was very aware of the phone in her pocket when she said that. She felt like it might come alive and laugh at her.

Ruby said "Well, a bit of stealing's alright for a good cause. Not that you'd ever steal anything Shiny Spar... I mean Lily. I tell you, if I ever find who stole my phone. I'll kill them. My dad gave it to me. I see him this weekend. If I haven't got it back by then he'll kill me."

At that moment Ruby looked like a shadow came from inside her and covered her face. Lily realised Ruby was really, really dreading her dad finding out she'd lost her phone.

Lily was trying to take it all in. Ruby didn't think she bullied Lily. She didn't realise how it upset her. She hadn't meant to destroy her castle. She hadn't even realised it was just hers. And, what's more Lily was really *liking* how Ruby was adding glitter and sticky silver paper. She had to admit, it looked good.

"What shall we call the castle?" Said Ruby

"Um…" said Lily

"The Castle of Um. Love it!" Said Ruby

Lily laughed. 'The Castle of Um' felt just right.

"I like it too" said Lily

And they worked quietly together for a few minutes on their castle, adding a sign to the front: 'The Castle of Um'

Lily said "I really don't like you going on about my blinking. Even if you didn't mean to be horrible. I feel bullied. So I think that means it's bullying. Please stop"

"Well, I'm sorry then. And I'll stop. No problemodonut"

Lily rather liked how Ruby said things like 'No ploblemodonut'. They chatted about the annoying supply teachers they had

had. It turned out Ruby missed Mr Hipkin too.

It was now or never thought Lily. She reached into her pocket, took out the phone and put it in front of Ruby.

It All Comes Out

"I'm really, really sorry" said Lily as she put the phone on the table.

Lily thought Ruby would be pleased or at least say 'That's okay'. After all they were having a nice chat. Becoming friends.

But Ruby didn't react like that. Instead, she turned round and pushed Lily with all her strength in the chest so Lily went stumbling backwards, knocking down chairs and tables. Ruby screamed "IT WAS YOU!!" and came towards Lily with her fist raised as she tried to get up from the floor.

At that moment there was a voice from behind them. "STOP THIS! WHAT IS GOING ON?"

They looked up to see Mr Hipkin standing in the doorway.

Mr Hipkin took Lily and Ruby to Mrs Standhope's office.

Lily couldn't stop talking. It felt good to talk even though the worst thing *ever* was happening. If she was going to get permanently excluded she might as well enjoy this moment of getting all her worries out. She talked and talked about the bullying, the stealing, the burying, the lost ring, the stinky bin, the digging up in the moonlight, the foxes, Moses' presents (cute), the castle and the glitter…on and on she went while the others looked on in stunned silence.

Lily said "Ruby didn't mean to bully me but maybe Ruby could just think before she says nasty things"

And then I guess she was in a bit of a muddle because she turned to Mr Hipkin and said "I'm glad your nose is back"

Ruby was so stunned by hearing what silent-perfect-goody-goody-shiny-two-shoes had been up to that she had forgotten to be angry. There were sorrys all round, before Mrs Standhope and Mr Hipkin even got round to asking them to say aplogise to each other. Lily said she was sorry about the phone again. Ruby said she was sorry about the teasing and the pushing- though she secretly thought that Lily deserved that push. They talked through everything for the whole afternoon. They talked about how Ruby should think before she said nasty things or shoved people when she was angry. And they talked about how Lily could be brave and talk to teachers if she had problems. And Mr Hipkin and Mrs Standhope said they knew it had been difficult having all those supply teachers.

Despite being through so much, Ruby's phone hummed into life when they turned it on. It was as good as new.

Funny Friends

Lily and Ruby both got lunch time detentions for a week. But Mr Hipkin said they had to work on the castle together during this time. Lily grew to really enjoy Ruby's crazy, just-stick-things-on-without-thinking way of doing the castle. She also liked how Ruby made her laugh.

One day Ruby bought her in an old comic 'Beano' book, full of crazy comic strips. She'd bought it because of the last page- an amazing detailed picture spread over a double page. It was a picture of a pink fairy tale castle. It was full of details of princesses and knights doing funny things. Like a princess marrying a dragon while the knight looked on grumpily. Lily

found she could look at it for hours. It made her laugh. Quietly. Inside.

Ruby could be really kind without thinking. She could also be really mean without thinking- like picking on Lily about her blinking. Just-doing-things-without-thinking was part of who Ruby was. And Lily grew to like it.

Ruby liked how Lily was really good at cutting and sticking neatly. And she loved how she was calm and listened to her talk about anything she wanted to. It was easy to talk to Lily. There was no one else she could talk to like she could talk to Lily. Lily wasn't shouty and jokey all the time like her other friends. They ended up talking about all the teachers, their parents, and their friends. They decided to invite James to join them to play with them both at Lily's house next Saturday.

The Journey On

Lily breathed in the wild night air,

At last, she was back on the roof.

She noticed a wheel, like you'd find on a ship,

She turned it, and the whole castle moved.

Lily skilfully steered her castle up high,

Over clouds and planes flying by,

She nearly bumped into Mr Hipkin the wizard,

As he waved from his flying pear pie.

She flew to England and to her home town,

And to her own school way below,

Where Ruby, James and all of her friends,

Were waiting outside to go home.

She saw that this story, when seen from up high,

Was a small part of her journey of life.

She waggled her finger, and felt her wild strength-

The strength to be brave, wise, and kind.

Now she flew on, to those million moons,

But returned to her bed every night.

You can imagine the places she found,

And write your own book, if you like...

...write your own book, if you like.